The
BLEACHER BIBLE

The True Fan's Guide
To Better Heckling

BY CHRIS SNEAD

COTTEN PUBLISHING COMPANY
LUBBOCK, TEXAS

This book is dedicated to my Mom and Dad.

ISBN: 0-925854-16-6

Cotten Publishing Company
P.O. Box 16243
Lubbock, Texas 79490

First Edition

Thanks to Bob Snead for the illustrations on Pages 37, 45, & 67.

Printed and bound in the United States of America

FOREWORD

DAN LAW Field. To the growing numbers of fans of Texas Tech Red Raider Baseball and those who follow the new Lubbock Crickets minor league franchise that name has deep meaning. I remember this baseball park before the Raiders played the great game under lights, and I remember it before the Department of Athletics installed the turf infield and the magnificent scoreboard beyond the fence in center-right field. Dan Law Field's expanse was sacred then, without those modern trappings, and its acres remain sacred to this day. I cannot, however, remember Dan Law Field without Chris Snead, the author of this compilation and the most visible of the fans who haunt this park every year between February and September.

My earliest memory of Chris dates back to a chilly, blustery Friday night in March 1989. I was a freshman at Texas Tech and attending my first Red Raider baseball game, a contest against the Wyoming Cowboys. Early in the game the officials ejected the Cowboys' coach for some reason I don't remember. What I do remember was Chris, who strolled to the end of the grandstand and leaned over the railing in order to speak to the hapless coach, who was sitting in a folding chair behind the visitors' dugout. With much concern evident in his voice, Chris said: "What's the matter, coach, can't see the game?" Though I was aware that baseball—from the little leagues to the Major Leagues—had boisterous and often outspoken fans, this was my first direct experience with what I have come to know and love as heckling.

In the six years since then, over the course of dozens of Red Raider and Lubbock Crickets baseball games, I have grown to have a better appreciation not only of the game of baseball itself, but also of being a student and fan of the game. Much of this is due to heckling, and sometimes just watching the game, with Chris and some of the other devotees who often sit in the bleachers immediately behind home plate. These many fans share the memories of Texas Tech's rapid rise from being an aver-

3

age, third or fourth place squad in the Southwest Conference, to a consistent nationally-ranked team that annually challenges for the Conference championship and a coveted spot in the NCAA Tournament.

Among these great moments are victories over perennial powerhouses such as the Wichita State Shockers and the Oklahoma Sooners. Chris attended the latter game to cheer the Raiders on to victory on the day of his wedding to Sue, who is always there with him in the bleachers. There were impressive and long-awaited victories over Grand Canyon and Cliff Gustafson's Texas Longhorns, and these memories are rounded out by a fabulous road trip to Wichita, Kansas, where the number-one seeded Red Raiders made an impressive first-ever appearance in the NCAA Mid West Regional. Many other fans remember the summer of 1995, when the Lubbock Crickets won the Texas-Louisiana League Championship in the first year of their existence.

It is for these disciples of baseball that Chris has decided to compile this heckling fan's instruction manual. These pages, which in the not too distant past were nothing more than a ragged stack of 3 x 5 index cards, contain observations and wisdom from many sources and many fans collected over a span of years. The goal is not to produce obnoxious observers, but "educated" hecklers who can help provide the home team with a well-deserved home field advantage without crossing the boundaries of sportsmanship or good taste.

Compare this goal with the long history of heckling. As early as 1888 obnoxious fans were known as "kranks," and one observer in that year published a study of them entitled *The Krank: His Language and What It Means*. Baseball historian David Voigt wrote of the odious fan: "Kranks were incorrigible nuisances who would annoy fellow horsecar passengers enroute to a game. Bucking the line at the ticket window, they would impose themselves on both ticket seller and gatekeeper, with requests for inside 'dope.' Once inside the park, they would head for the newspaper pen to badger the writers . . . During the course of a game they would tirelessly shout advice to the players and scornful epithets to the umpires." The obnoxious fan developed with the game, and these "boo birds" would jeer the home team when it let them down, as well as heaping abuse on opposing teams' players. Voigt chronicles the game's more famous hecklers: "San Diego's 'tuba man' loaded his instrument with beer bottles, the contents of which soon inspired his blasts; Shea Stadium's 'sign man' carried a stack of some 700 critical signs for situationally harassing players, owners, umpires, and other fans; Philadelphia's 'umpire baiter' was said to be the vilest of fans; and Atlanta's 'rabble rouser' fired up fans much better than he did the forlorn Braves . . . Jeering 'bleacher bums' at Wrigley Field wore yellow helmets,

4

doused enemy players with drinks, and blew bugles . . ."

The Braves have since improved, and with this guide, so can your heckling. Friendly and inspired teasing of the visiting team within the bounds of good taste can add to the enjoyment of the total baseball atmosphere while it helps the home team.

The goal is also to entertain, because baseball, though it is many things to many people, is wonderfully entertaining to all who are true fans. The entertainment is not just in the game itself, but in the entire ballpark experience. Successful baseball entrepreneurs have always known this. Legendary owner and promoter Bill Veeck, who brought the Cleveland Indians their first world championship in 1948, was wise enough to do his marketing research among the rabid Tribe fans in the "cheap seats." Chris compiled this book for all the fans who come to Dan Law Field, or any ballpark where the Boys of Summer play. Whether you sit in the cheap seats, the press box, or even the dugout, you can be a part of the total baseball experience.

Enjoy Chris' labor of love, and bring it often to Dan Law Field or to whatever ballpark you call home to cheer the Red Raiders, the Lubbock Crickets, or the team of your choice on to victory. Go Tech!

LES CULLEN
Lubbock, Texas
November 1995

INTRODUCTION

A ND on the eighth day, God created baseball. A few minutes later, to make it more interesting, He created hecklers. Some people think heckling is easy. They think it's something anyone can do. Heckling, at its best, is a form of art. It is part of the game, but it is not for everyone. It is not for the squeamish or the weak-of-spirit. It is not a part-time chore (mainly because if you're good, they'll want you back for the next game). Simply put, heckling is not just sitting on the front row shooting off a bunch of insults. Heckling is using whatever persuasive measures you can to throw a player off his game. The object of heckling is to get the players on the field thinking about you more than they are thinking about the game. Heckling is baseball—or at least it is as much a part of baseball as chewing tobacco: one of those things people don't necessarily like but accept as a part of the game.

Believe it or not, the players hear what is being said. They may not hear all of it clearly, but they hear it. Which is why you will want to keep a close eye on what it is you are actually saying. It can be the difference between going home after the game and going home after the game minus several of your teeth. In this age of players attacking fans and fans berating players, we need to have a set of unbreakable rules—commandments, if you will—to follow when we heckle our brethren.

COMMANDMENT I: *THOU SHALT NOT USE PROFANITY.*
Remember this one thing, baseball is still a family sport.
Fathers and sons, mom and dad, the whole family.
Nobody wants to hear you spouting off a bunch of @#$&%!

COMMANDMENT II: *THOU SHALT NOT INSULT THE MOTHER.*
This should be obvious. What good could come from saying something about someone else's mother? Is that what we want? I don't think so. Leave mom out of it.
We don't need any of this garbage at our games. We want people to appreciate what we do, not resent us for it.

COMMANDMENT III: *THOU SHALT BE INTELLIGENT.*

Do I really need to explain this? Know what you are talking about. Remember, credibility lends respect to your task.

COMMANDMENT IV: *THOU SHALT LOVE BASEBALL.*

Is there any doubt about this? Who in this great country would disparage America's pastime? If you don't love baseball, what are you doing here?

COMMANDMENT V: *THOU SHALT BE AWARE OF THE PEOPLE AROUND YOU.*

This is a really touchy one. Even though some of the funniest stuff you have may be about overweight guys or bald guys, the person next to you may not think it's terribly funny.

COMMANDMENT VI: *THOU SHALT BE WITTY.*

Only one rule to remember here: if you are the only one laughing, it wasn't funny.

COMMANDMENT VII: *THOU SHALT NOT OVERKILL.*

Listen, if somebody does something funny in the first inning, you should not keep ragging on it in the fifth. The more you say something, the less effective it becomes. You must be aware that the same stuff gets really old after a couple of games—especially in a series against the same team. Unless something is really working on one or two guys, put it away for a couple or three games.

COMMANDMENT VIII: *THOU SHALT BE FRIENDLY.*

The best way to make those guys listen to you and divert their attention from the task at hand is to be just as nice as you can be. When you look into the dugout, wave and say, "Hi guys!"

COMMANDMENT IX: *THOU SHALT NOT CROSS THE LINE.*
That line is the line of brutality. Look, the players know
that heckling is part of the game. Don't make it personal
between you and the players. Remember, they have bats,
you don't.

COMMANDMENT X: *THOU SHALT REMEMBER THE CHILDREN.*
No matter what you want to believe about role models,
the children are watching and listening. They hear what
you say and see what you do. Be aware of that when you
sit in the stands. If you don't know whether you fit the bill,
just ask yourself, would you want your best friend's
kid sister or brother to sit next to you at the ball game?
Well, would you?

Look, let's be honest, heckling isn't for everyone; in fact, it is for very few people.
You've got to be a little funny, a little smart, part psychologist, a little daring and
willing to accept whatever repercussions that may result. If you think you're up to it,
then get out to the ballpark and make some friends on the opposing team.

Table of Contents

CHAPTER 1

Fat Guys

Fat Guys

What can you say about these guys? They don't miss many meals. And they never met a jelly doughnut they didn't like. Hey, maybe it's just a thyroid problem! Then again maybe they just need to go on a diet. Oh my goodness, these guys are killin' me . . . What a joke! Some of my favorites over the years have been P. D. Neff from the University of Nebraska-Kearney (formerly Kearney State) and the Duke, Duke Gonzales, from Eastern New Mexico. There was also the guy from Hardin-Simmons whose name escapes me. I ragged him and his dad came over. He told me I could gain a few pounds myself and I told him that apple didn't fall far from the tree. The rest of the day is kind of fuzzy after that.

Fat Guys—

"Your butt looks like 150 pounds of bubble gum! Please don't blow a bubble!"

KEVIN NELSON, Kansas City, Missouri

"You're fat!"

"... And now batting ... [The Goodyear Blimp, Fat Albert, The Michelin Man, The Pillsbury Dough Boy, Bob's Big Boy]."

"It's PB Max ... the PB stands for Pretty Big ... [or] the PB stands for Portly Ballplayer."

"Chunky"

"You look like Jell-O with ears!"

KEVIN NELSON, Kansas City, Missouri

"Eat a carrot"

"Go on a diet!"

"Just say no ... to seconds!"

"There's a cheeseburger on second!"

RAGGER UNKNOWN

"Oxygen! Get him some oxygen. Call a physician."

"Oh no! He's gonna fall!"

"Have you been stealing your teammates' meal tickets again?"

RAGGER UNKNOWN

Fat Guys—

"It's O.K. to pull a piano, as long as you don't stop to play it!"
RANDY DUROSS,
Texas Tech Baseball Player

"Hit the Sizzler after the ballgame . . . all you can eat!"
SCOTT GOWER, Lubbock, Texas

"What size are those pants—Large, Extra Large, or Oh My God, it's comin' at us?"
ANDREW DICE CLAY, Comedian

"When you go into a 7-11, is it a 6-10 when you come out?"
UPTOWN COMEDY CLUB, Comedian Unknown

"Is that a calzone in your back pocket?"
SCOTT GOWER, Lubbock, Texas

"When you go to the zoo, do the animals try to feed you?"
UPTOWN COMEDY CLUB

"You're so fat, you could use a Hula Hoop to hold up your pants."
UPTOWN COMEDY CLUB

"Did you get your uniform at Tents-R-Us?"
RAGGER UNKNOWN

"Are those two uniforms sewn together?"
RAGGER UNKNOWN

Fat Guys–

"Do you eat until you're full or until you're tired?"

"Does the turf keep you from grazing?"

"You're so fat, if you broke your leg, gravy would spill out."
UPTOWN COMEDY CLUB, Comedian Unknown

"You're so fat you can't wear an 'X' jacket or helicopters would try to land on your back."
UPTOWN COMEDY CLUB

"Hey Snack Bar! Get that hamburger out of your pocket!"
Fan, to Tony Gwynn

"They say you lost weight . . . you look like you're all the way down to 289!"
BRUCE JENKINS, Baseball Player

"A fat tub of goo . . . you're the fattest man in collegiate sports!"
DAVID LETTERMAN

"You look like a man trying to conceal a ham under your shirt!"
GARY PETERSON, Journalist

"I saw you in New York last Thanksgiving. You were a blimp in Macy's Parade."
STEVE SAX, Baseball Player

"If they could make a curve ball look like a cheeseburger, you would be batting 1.000!"

Fat Guys—

"I could stay in great shape running laps around your waist."

"You're pullin' the moon out of orbit!"

"Weebles Wobble but they don't fall down."
                                    TELEVISION COMMERCIAL

"Call Greenpeace. We have a beached whale on the mound."
                                    TEXAS A&M RAGGIES

"Is that a blowhole under your cap?"
                                    TEXAS A&M RAGGIES

CHAPTER 2

Short Guys

Short Guys

I love these guys because they're the only ones on the team with a sense of humor. They must have one if they think they're going to get a shot to play in today's game. At any rate, what is it with these guys? Every team has one or two, runnin' around the coach's ankles, gettin' in the way. And they've always got a chip on their shoulder. I guess I would too if the world had dealt me a height of 4' 11". What most of them lack in height they usually make up in character. Which is good because a lot of teams lack character. You'll find these mighty mites on the rosters of most of the Ma and Pa universities scattered across this great land of ours. Schools with 'Christian' in the name. The truth hurts short guys.

Short Guys—

"Stand up!"

"Get him a high chair!"

"Get him a batter's mound!"

KEVIN NELSON, Kansas City, Missouri

"Check his I.D. . . . I don't think he's old enough."

"Is this your class field trip?"

"Let's see your permission slip."

"Did you get on the wrong bus this morning? Maybe you should be at the museum with the other fourth graders."

"Isn't it past your bedtime?"

"Get him a lighter bat."

"Who made your uniform . . . Garanimals?"

SCOTT GOWER, Lubbock, Texas

"I've got warts bigger than you."

KEVIN NELSON, Kansas City, Missouri

"I lost you behind the pitcher's mound."

RAGGER UNKNOWN

Short Guys—

"If your uniform had pinstripes, yours would only have one!"

RAGGER UNKNOWN

"Midget!"

"Amoeba!"

"Squirt!"

"Squirt! I really mean it!"

"Little Man!"

"Pipsqueak!"

"Button your diaper!"

RAGGER UNKNOWN

"Give him a pacifier!"

"Whaaaaaaaaaaaa!"

"Your shoes are so small, you can't even give 'em to Little Leaguers."

JAY JOHNSTONE, TV host

"You would make a great short stop but the grounders keep going over your head."

JOE SAMBITO, Baseball Player

Short Guys–

"Did they measure you while you were standing on the mound?"

TEXAS A&M RAGGIES

"Does your mom still dress you?"

TEXAS A&M RAGGIES

CHAPTER 3

Dugout Loudmouths

Dugout Loudmouths

You just gotta love these guys. They have the least amount of talent, the least amount of playing time, and the most to say from the bench. They also have the least to do with the outcome of the game—yet at the end they celebrate as though they scored the winning run. You know what they are: a bunch of cheerleaders! A bunch of no-playin', skirt wearin', pom-pon throwin' pine riders! Grab some bench, pal, and shut your mouth!

ℒoudmouths–

"You've been sittin' the bench so long your teammates call you 'Judge'!"

RAGGER UNKNOWN

"You've got a mouth like an outboard motor!"

"Quiet in the playpen!"

RAGGER UNKNOWN

"Dry up, cheerleaders!"

RAGGER UNKNOWN

"Let's see some leg, cheerleader!"

MIKE GUSTAFSON, Lubbock, Texas

"Break out the Pom-Pons, ladies!"

"There's no crying in baseball!"

TOM HANKS - A League Of Their Own

"Shut up, ring master!"

"How long does it take you to pull the pine needles out of your butt?"

TEXAS A&M RAGGIES

CHAPTER 4

Coaches' Sons

Coaches' Sons

Y ou have to feel kind of sorry for these guys because you know the only reason they made the team was because Pa Kettle was the coach. I don't know which is worse—the son realizing: "Uh oh, Dad's the only coach who's going to give me a scholarship!" or the dad realizing, "Uh oh, I'm the only guy dumb enough to give my kid a scholarship!" Oh well, that's the chance you took when you elected not to use a condom, Dad. This is not to say all coaches' sons are brutal. We've had two here in Lubbock and both of them were pretty good. That just means we were ahead of the Bell Curve. For the most part, you can see why these guys are playing for Dad.

Coaches' Sons—

"No wonder your dad gave you a scholarship!"

"Maybe your parents were hoping for a girl!"

SCOTT GOWER, Lubbock, Texas

"That's it! No dinner for you tonight."

"Go to your room. No dinner or TV tonight."

"Well Coach, you see what happens when you don't use a condom!"

"I think it's time for a father-daughter talk."

TEXAS A&M RAGGIES

CHAPTER 5

Mound Conferences

Mound Conferences

Well, well, well. The great conference on the hill. It's at this point everyone in the crowd thinks that some brilliant strategy is being devised by the coach and his players. Ba-loney. Those guys out there don't have a clue as to what they are gonna do. The catcher and pitcher are probably afraid to pitch to the guy at the plate. Heck, the coach probably is too.

Mound Conferences—

"Break up the tea party, ladies!"

"O.K., for the last time, one's a fast ball, two's a curve."

DANA DICK, San Angelo, Texas

"Well, what do you want to get coach for his birthday?"

"Where do you want to go for dinner?"

"Coach, they're laughin' at me . . . I don't wanna play anymore!"

"Candlesticks make a nice gift."

ROBERT WUHL – Bull Durham

"We need a live rooster to take the hex off of _____'s glove."

KEVIN COSTNER – Bull Durham

CHAPTER 6

Umpires

Umpires

As one of the few, the proud, the brave men who wear the blue, I can't say that these guys are not doing a great job. I want everyone to know that I would never use any of these rags on my brethren. It just wouldn't be right. Well, I wouldn't use any of 'em in a game where I knew the umpires. But seriously, you have to feel for the boys in blue. They have a tough job, and whether you want to believe it or not, they do it well. Most umpires are seriously doing the best job they can. This is not to say that they all have a clue. Some of these guys are idiots and how they got the authority to run a baseball game truly escapes me.

Umpires–

"Why don't you get your seeing-eye dog to call it for you?"

"Why don't you poke a hole in that mask?"

SCOTT PATTERSON, Lubbock, Texas

"That plate's got corners you know . . . I saw your wife standing on it last night!"

KEVIN COSTNER – Bull Durham

"I'm not questioning your effort, Blue . . . I'm questioning your eyesight!"

TOMMY LASORDA, Manager

"Tell me, Ump, how can you sleep with all these lights on?"

AMOS OTIS, Baseball Player

"If you're just gonna watch the game, why don't you buy a ticket?"

"Stevie W on der could see that one, Blue."

"You're missin' a great game, Blue!"

"First guy to lay a finger on the old blind man is off the team!"

GENE MAUCH, Manager

"You umpires must be staying at the Holiday Inn 'cause that's the only hotel in town with Braille numbers on the elevators."

EARL WEAVER, Manager

CHAPTER 7

Brutal Hitters

Brutal Hitters

As the saying goes, baseball is a non-contact sport, but some guys seem to take that literally. Many of these guys are still looking for the first or second hit of their careers. The truth is, they're really just not good hitters. For them, the Mendoza Line (.200) is no more than a pipe dream. There's not much you can say about these guys because when they're batting, we spend three-fourths of the time laughing at them.

Brutal Hitters—

"You've got jungle disease: you look like Tarzan but you swing like Jane."

JASON ARCHINAL, Lubbock, Texas

"You've got a case of the zactlies . . . you swing zactly like a woman!"

BONNIE SMITH, El Paso, Texas

"Baseball is supposed to be a non-contact sport, but you seem to take it literally!"

LARRY DOUGHTY, Pirates' General Manager

"You couldn't hit a home run if you were standing on second base!"

DON ZIMMER, Rockies Coach

"You couldn't hit water if you fell out of a boat."

"You couldn't hit sand if you fell off a camel."

RUBE – Major League

"Close your eyes and swing—it'll improve your chances."

TEXAS A&M RAGGIES

"You look like a victim!"

TEXAS A&M RAGGIES

CHAPTER 8

Brutal Fielders

Brutal Fielders

E very once in a while there comes along a guy they call the next Ozzie Smith, or the next Barry Larkin, Pee Wee Reese, or Phil Rizzuto. Unfortunately, these guys don't have anything to worry about. I like to call these guys my "Tony Lama" players, because any time these guys touch the ball . . . BOOT!

Brutal Fielders—

"When you field the ball, it sounds like Big Ben at 10 o'clock—Bong!"
ROLLIE FINGERS, Baseball Pitcher

"You've got all the defensive skills of the Lincoln Tunnel!"
RON LUCIANO, Umpire

"You're a Williams-type player—you bat like Ted but you field like Esther!"
Sportswriter, talking about Dick Stuart

"You could be a great shortstop but all the grounders keep bouncin' over your head."
Baseball's Greatest Insults

"Some of your fielders must be allergic to the ball."
DICK DRAGO, Baseball Pitcher

"You never got acquainted with your glove and never met a ground ball that you liked."
PAUL RICHARDS, Manager

"Is it true that when you tried to commit suicide by jumping in front of a bus it went through your legs?"
WALLY PHILLIPS, Broadcaster

"When they list the great fielders of all time, you'll be there listening."
CASEY STENGEL, Manager

Brutal Fielders–

"You've got all the range of the Bird Man of Alcatraz."

BILL JAMES, Author

"You change your infield more than your underwear."

BILL JAMES

"Your infield has more holes than a porcupine's underwear."

BILL JAMES

"I've seen better hands on a clock!"

TEXAS A&M RAGGIES

CHAPTER 9

Brutal Teams

Brutal Teams

At this point in the original book, I made a list of some of the worst baseball teams I had ever laid eyes on, but my publisher told me I would be sued in such a way that it would not be comfortable to my wallet. So in the interest of fiscal prudence, let's just say that there are some baseball clubs out there that you and I along with eight to ten nuns could beat on any given afternoon.

Brutal Teams—

"You guys took batting practice earlier and the pitching machine threw a no-hitter."

"Other teams win and make it look easy; you guys lose and make it look hard."

DAVID BRINKLEY, Commentator

"The latest diet is better than Jenny Craig—you only eat when you win."

GEORGE SHEARING, Pianist

"How about the new _____ soup? Two sips and you choke."

POPULAR JOKE

"Rooting for you guys is like rooting for Iraq. You might win one every once in a while, but you know in the end you're gonna get crushed."

STEVE COZZENS, Columnist

"You guys play like King Kong one day and like Fay Wray the next."

TERRY KENNEDY, Manager

"You guys are four players from being a good team—and the four players are named Mickey, Babe, Lou and Yogi."

BILL ROBINSON, Baseball Player

"At the rate you guys are going, a two out walk is a rally."

STUMP MERRILL, Manager

Brutal Teams–

"If there was a new way to lose, you guys would discover it."

JOE GARAGIOLA, Player/Commentator

"The truth is, you guys just aren't a very good team."

JERRY CRASNICK

"You guys lack identity. Your colors should be beige."

JERRY CRASNICK

"I don't know which is worse, watching this game or playing in it."

TERRY KENNEDY, Baseball Player

"You guys started off historically bad and then went into a slump!"

JOHN MILLER, Broadcaster

"Why don't you take up crochet?—make yourselves a nice sweater."

JASON ARCHINAL, Lubbock, Texas

"Turn in your scholarship."

"Maybe baseball's not your sport."

"Your teammates are laughin' at you."

"Are you a baseball team or a circus act?"

"I bet your parents are pretty embarrassed."

Brutal Teams–

"Where's the ringmaster? Where's the bearded lady?"

"We're whipping you like a rented mule."

"I looked up baseball player in the dictionary and it said 'not you'."

RAGGER UNKNOWN

"It's like a bad game of Scrabble; you can't do anything with a bunch of E's and K's."

BRIAN CUTTER, Lubbock, Texas

"You've got a lot of triple-threat men—slip, fumble and fall!"

JOE GARAGIOLA

CHAPTER 10

Bad Base Runners

Bad Base Runners

Carl Lewis, Leroy Burrell, Ben Johnson . . . not these guys. By every stretch of the imagination, we will see that not everyone was made to be fleet of foot.

Bad Base Runners–

"Unhitch the trailer."

"You're pulling a trailer with a piano in it."

"Someone call U-Haul. One of their longbed, wide-body vans is on the loose!"

"You look like a greyhound, but you run like a bus."

GEORGE BRETT, Baseball Player

"How could someone who runs as slow as you pull a muscle?"

PETE ROSE, former Baseball Player/Manager

"You run too long in one place."

DIZZY DEAN, Pitcher

"You've got a lot of up and down but not much forward."

"You're so slow, you couldn't tag up on a fly ball to San Antonio!"

SPORTSWRITER

"I could take sequence photos of you with a Polaroid camera."

RON LUCIANO, Umpire

"You're like a human rain delay."

"I could time you with a sundial."

Bad Base Runners—

"The turf is growing."

"Tumbleweeds roll uphill faster than you run."

"You just run until you're out."

TIM SULLIVAN, Sportswriter

"My nose runs faster than you!"

RAGGER UNKNOWN

You run slower than a fat girl chasing a Chihuahua up a staircase."

BILL JAMES, Author

STUPID!"

TEXAS A&M RAGGIES

CHAPTER 11

Brutal Players

Brutal Players

To be completed by the reader.

Brutal Players—

"You're brutal."

"You're horrible."

"You're terrible."

"You're pathetic . . . P-A-thetic!"

"Get a clue!"

"Go to the bank, take out a loan, and go buy a clue!"

"Are you really playin' baseball or are you just usin' The Force?"

RAGGER UNKNOWN

"If brains were dynamite, you wouldn't have enough to blow your nose!"

"You're about as useful as a porcupine in a nudist colony."

CHAPTER 12

Brutal Pitchers

...and Catchers

Brutal Pitchers

Every team has at least one; some teams have a whole staff of them. Brutal pitchers. No matter how many runs ahead you are, no matter how bad the team you're playing, this guy is not even gonna sniff the field. Some coaches have a full staff of these guys—they'll tell you. It's like back in grade school and the last guy to get selected for a game—you know, the really bad one; well, that kid is all grown up now and playing college baseball . . . and trying to pitch!

Brutal Pitchers–

"How are you gonna get outta this one, Houdini?"

"Hurry, hurry . . . step right up and get a walk!"

"Boy, that last pitch got outta here in a hurry!"

"Anything that goes that far should have a stewardess on it!"

"Why don't you get a running start?"

"You're interfering with air traffic."

"You're committing suicide out there. Call Dr. Kevorkian!"

WAYNE BERNIER, Lubbock, Texas

"Someone go out there and put another quarter in the pitcher."

"Wind him up again, Coach!"

"You ought to be a drum major."

"You should sign on with Merrill Lynch in honor of your ERA. It's so high that when stockbrokers hear it, they go SELL, SELL!"

TONY KORNHEISER, Columnist

"Your pitches have the velocity of a falling leaf."

Brutal Pitchers—

"You ought to wear a disclaimer on your back that says, 'Allow four to six weeks for delivery."

GARY PETERSON, Columnist

"Some speed guns have been clocked at 45 mph."

UNIDENTIFIED BROADCASTER

"You've walked more people than a seeing eye dog."

FRANK LUKSA, Sportswriter

"You're the only pitcher in baseball that they time with a sundial."

MICKEY MANTLE, Baseball Player

"The only good thing about you is that you're the same whether you're good or bad. The only thing is, you don't know the difference."

BILLY CONNORS

"You're a rotator cuff operation waiting to happen."

"Your deck is missing all of the face cards."

GORMAN THOMAS, Baseball Player

"I"ve seen better arms on a chair."

RAGGER UNKNOWN

"You couldn't strike out a match."

Brutal Pitchers–

"You couldn't strike ME out."

"You needed a cutoff man for that pitch."

"Stop. You're killing the worms!"

KEVIN NELSON, Kansas City, Missouri

"You throw like a girl!"

Movie: "The Sandlot"

"Rag Arm."

"Meat! Serve it up!"

"You're choking—I can see the rope burns around your neck."

"Stick a fork in him. He's done!"

"And for my next trick…"

KIRK WINTERROWD, Austin, Texas

...and Catchers—

"You couldn't catch a cold standing naked in a snowstorm!"

"Maybe you're left-handed."

SCOTT GOWER, Lubbock, Texas

"You're a backstop."

KIRK WINTERROWD, Austin, Texas

"You couldn't throw me out if I crawled backwards to second."

"Are you transparent? . . . maybe he can't see you back there!"

JASON ARCHINAL, Lubbock, Texas

"Who ever called you a catcher?"

Glossary of Baseball Terms

A

ADJUST — What a batter must do in order to escape the hecklers in the front row. Since most batters are not able to do this, they end up back on the bench with a big OUT tattooed on their forehead.

A.R.B.Y. — Already By You. An expression used to point out a player's ineptitude with the bat.

B

BACKSTOP — 1. Structure erected behind the catcher to keep the ball from hitting the fans. 2. Slang term for catcher.

BALL — Round, white orb used to play the game.

BASE — One of the three safe havens on the way to the scoring plate. It is the objective of the player to reach these havens safely.

BASEBALL — The game we live for.

BATTER'S BOX — Where the batter stands and attempts to hit the offering from the pitcher.

BENCH — The place where those with little or no talent spend their time during the game.

BLEACHERS — The place where all of the fans sit.

BLUE — Another term for the umpire.

BLIND — What half of the people in the stands think the umpire is. The other half believe he's just an idiot.

BOMB — Home run.

BONUS CANTOS — Slang term meaning Extra Innings. Some believe when a game goes into extra innings it means a bonus for the fans because they are getting more for their money.

BRAILLE — The medium many people believe is used by umpires to enable them to read.

BRUSH BACK — Method used by the pitcher to establish ownership of the plate. In rare cases, brush back pitches result in a Home Run on the next pitch or a fight on the same pitch.

BRUTAL — Description of a player who is less than average. Terrible. Horrible.

BULL PEN — Where the relief pitcher goes to warm up. Many people believe the relief pitcher will magically be able to save the game but in reality, if you are using these guys, you are in deep kimshee.

BUS DRIVER — The person in control of the bus during a road trip, sometimes the head coach.

ℭ

CATCHER — The player assigned to receive the pitch from the pitcher. Sometimes referred to as a backstop.

CENTER FIELD — The middle portion of the outfield where the center fielder plays.

CHEERLEADERS — Players who sit the bench and cheer on their team because they are not good enough to play. These are normally the players with the biggest mouths.

CHIN MUSIC *[sometimes called Symphony]* — A pitch thrown so as to just miss the batter's head right under the chin.

CHUNKY — Colorful term describing some of the more obese players.

CIRCLE CHANGE — A really hard pitch to throw or hit.

CLEAN UP — The fourth batter in the lineup.

CONFERENCE — What happens when the catcher or coach goes out to visit the pitcher. Sometimes this is a stalling tactic because they know the batter is going to tattoo anything the pitcher throws.

CORNER — 1. The black portion of the plate. 2. First or Third Base on a baseball field.

CRO-MAGNON MAN — Early man who probably did not play baseball.

CUT-OFF MAN — 1. A player assigned to get in between the person throwing the ball and the person who is receiving the ball in order to make sure the ball gets delivered to the most desirable position. 2. The person who gets between the pitcher and catcher to make sure a Howard Payne pitch gets across the plate.

DEUCE— Slang term for curve ball.

DEFENSE— The objective of the nine guys who play together in the field.

DIAMOND— 1. The shape of the field on which the game of baseball is played. 2. A very expensive rock.

DICTIONARY— A book that many college students own but seldom use.

DONG— A Home Run.

DOUBLE — When a player gets two bases on a single hit.

DOUBLE PLAY — What happens when a team gets two outs on a single hit.

Ɛ

EN FUEGO — Spanish for On Fire.

ERROR — When someone makes a mistake that allows the opposing team to move without getting a hit.

E.R.A. — Earned Run Average. A pitcher's "grade" or "rating." Based on the number of runs allowed to the opposition without errors over nine innings.

EXPLOIT — What a lot of coaches do to their players while they are on scholarship.

Ƒ

FAST BALL — A pitch that most high school kids can hit and many college kids can't.

FEAR — What the batter has when the first pitch is over his head.

FIELD — The place where a baseball game is played.

FIRST BASE — The place that many college players have never seen. The first stop on the way to Home Plate.

FLARE — What the pitcher should send up when he is throwing to first base.

G

GAS — Slang term for a fast ball.

GILOOLEY — When a pitch hits a batter in the shin.

GIMP — An injured player.

GOOSE EGG — When a team fails to get a run in an inning or a game.

GRASS — What a real baseball field has somewhere on it.

GREYHOUND — 1. Bus line that carries many teams to baseball events. 2. The mascot of Eastern New Mexico University.

GROUNDER — When a batter hits a ball and it scoots along the ground before the fielder picks it up.

H

HANGING CURVE — A curve ball that starts out too high and never breaks.

HEATER — Another term for fast ball.

HIT — When the batter successfully places the ball in a location that none of the fielders can reach in time to make a put out.

HOME RUN — When the batter hits the ball over the fence or reaches home plate before he can be put out by the defense.

HOSE — A player with tremendous arm strength and accuracy.

HURLER — Slang term for pitcher.

I

INFIELD — The area where the first, second, and third basemen, along with the shortstop, pitcher and catcher are stationed during a game.

INFIELD FLY — 1. When there is a runner on first and second, or when the bases are loaded with less than two outs and a batter hits a ball in the air that can be caught with ordinary effort. 2. The distance many small guys can hit the ball to.

INNING — The breakdown of a baseball game. Like quarters without time limits. In a normal game there are 9 innings.

INTERFERENCE — When a runner gets in the way of the fielder trying to field the ball.

J

JENNY CRAIG — A weight program that uses alternative food habits to encourage its participants to lose weight.

JERK — Someone who doesn't think heckling is funny.

JUMBO — A really big elephant-like player.

JUNIOR — When your name is the same as your father's.

JUXTAPOSITION — A word I defy most college students to define, or find another word it resembles.

K

K — The way to record a strikeout in the scorebook.

KING KONG — A large gorilla that stalked and took over New York City in a movie of the same name.

KNUCKLE BALL — A method of throwing the ball in which there is little or no rotation on the ball so as to throw off the timing of the batter.

£

LOLLYGAGGER — A player who doesn't hustle.

LEG THEORY — In Cricket, the way to brush back a batter by throwing at his legs.

LINE DRIVE — A base hit that flies by the infield without hitting the ground.

LONG BALL — A home run.

LOOPER — A hanging pitch or the result of that pitch into the outfield.

M

MASK — Metal shield worn by the catcher and the home plate umpire to protect their faces. In some cases, the mask is for the protection of the fans in the stands.

MEAL TICKET — The way many players' lunches and dinners are paid for. Sometimes a player will use not only his own meal ticket but those of several smaller teammates as well.

MEAT — A pitcher who has nothing. Nothing at all.

MOUND — The raised portion of the infield where the pitcher stands, designed to give him an advantage over the batters.

MONGO — That really big guy playing first base.

N

NO-HITTER — When the pitcher does not allow the opposing team a hit during the course of the game.

NO NO — 1. Slang term for a no-hitter. 2. Umpire Tim Henderson's way to call "Ball."

NONE — No one. Nothing. Zero.

NUN — A very religious woman who lives in a convent.

O

OFFENSE — What the team batting is trying to achieve.

OGRE — A really big ugly guy.

OUT — What the team in the field is trying to achieve.

OUTFIELD —Where the Left, Center, and Right fielders play.

PEA — A hard hit ball or a home run.

PEON —The guy who has to wash all of the jockstraps after the game.

PIANO — What those guys pullin' a trailer are hauling.

PIN STRIPES — Uniform design in which little vertical lines decorate the uniform from top to bottom. Some small players only have one.

PITCHER — The player who attempts to throw the ball in such a way that he causes the batter to miss, hit poorly, or pop up.

PITCHING MACHINE — Sometimes the best pitcher on the team. Sometimes the only guy that can get a ball across the plate.

PLATE — The white thing that looks like a house near where the catcher and umpire stand.

PLAYPEN — Also known as the dugout. The place where the benchwarmers sit.

POM-PON —What the cheerleaders in the dugout use to pep up the guys who actually play the game.

PRACTICE — Something many teams look like they do not do.

PRIZES — What you win on a game show.

PUT OUT — When the ball reaches the base before the slow runner does.

Q

QUACK — What the mascot of the University of Oregon says.

QUICHE — A meatless concoction my wife tries to get me to eat.

QUIT — What most teams do after the second inning against Wichita State.

R

RAG ARM — A pitcher that is not very good.

RAGGER — An extremely obnoxious, annoying person who sits on the front row and voices disparaging remarks toward the opposing team. Usually accompanied by two or three others.

RALLY — What happens when the team behind in the score begins to mount an effort to come back. For some teams, a two out walk is a rally.

RANGE — The amount of ground a fielder can cover from the time that the ball leaves the bat until the time he catches it.

ROOKIE — A player in his first year of service in a given level of baseball.

ROTATOR CUFF — The muscle that ties the shoulder, arm and collar bone together. A tear in this muscle, if bad enough, can mean the end of a player's career.

RUN — 1. The way to get to another base. 2. A score. 3. What some weak players get when they snag their pantyhose on the bench.

S

SCHOLARSHIP — Room, board, tuition and books tendered to a person as a way to influence him to attend a university. Scholarships, in turn, allow the institution to bastardize the individual for four years. In some cases, a fifth year of bastardization will be added if the player suffers an injury. At the end of the scholarship, the player is cast off, never to be heard from again, so the institution can concentrate on bastardizing the next crop of young skulls full of mush.

SECOND BASE — 1. The intermediate position between first and third. 2. Sometimes referred to as the "keystone." 3. The only base with two defensive players protecting it.

SEEING EYE DOG — The individual actually calling the game.

SEEING EYE SINGLE — A ball that seems to know where it is going so that it just avoids the outstretched hands of the defense.

SHORTSTOP — The fielder who plays between second and third. Expected to have a strong throwing arm.

SIGNS — What the catcher uses to tell the pitcher what kind of pitch to throw. Sometimes the pitcher will forget the difference between One and Two.

SINKER — A pitch that appears to be a fast ball until it drops or sinks out of the strike zone, usually leaving the batter looking stupid.

SKIPPER — Slang term for the manager or coach.

SLAP — 1. A base hit. 2. The just deserts for a lewd comment to a woman.

SLIDER — A pitch disguised to look like a fast ball until it slides away from the batter.

SLOPPY — What most teams play like at the beginning of the season, especially those traveling south for Spring Training or Spring Break.

SMURF— 1. A small baseball player. 2. A small blue cartoon character.

STATUE — A person who stands in the batter's box and never makes a move to swing the bat.

STEAL — The act of taking a base from the defense before they can make a put out.

STRIKE — 1. Any ball that crosses the designated zone without being hit fairly or called by the umpire. 2. What happens when greedy players and owners cannot agree on how to split up a billion dollars.

STRIKE OUT — When a batter, in the course of an at bat, receives 3 strikes.

SUICIDE SQUEEZE — When a player on third breaks for home in the hope that the batter is able to lay down a bunt out of the reach of the catcher or pitcher. Called a "suicide squeeze" because the runner is dead if the batter misses the ball or doesn't bunt it far enough.

SUNDIAL — A device for measuring time with a marker to indicate elapsed time by measuring the sun's shadow as it moves across a dial. Sometimes used to time very slow persons.

TAIL — What every pitcher wants his curve ball to have.

TANTRUM — What some coaches throw when their team is losing or the umpire makes a bad call.

TATER — A home run.

TEA PARTY — A conference on the mound when all the defensive players meet to discuss strategy.

THROW HEAT — The best way for a skinny little kid from a small town to get a scholarship to a big university.

TRAILER — What very slow or very fat players are pulling behind them.

TRIPLE — When a player reaches third base on a single hit.

TWINKIE — Putting one of these on second base is the best way for a big chunky guy to get a double.

U

U-HAUL — A type of trailer fat guys pull behind them.

UMPIRE — The person or persons responsible for deciding balls and strikes, fair and foul balls, and outs and safes.

UNIFORMS — What players wear to distinguish one team from another.

V

VELOCITY — The rate of speed at which the ball travels.

VICTIM — A player who looks at strike three without swinging.

W

WALK — A free pass to first base when a batter receives four pitches judged to be out of the strike zone in a single at-bat.

WHEELS — Term for a baseball player's legs.

WHIFF — 1. The sound you hear when a batter swings and misses the ball completely. 2. A slang term for a strikeout.

X

X-RAY — Machine used by doctors to look at your insides.

Y

YELLOW — A primary color.

Z

ZACTLIES — When a person does something exactly like something else.

ZOO — 1. A place where lots of animals from around the world are collected so that people young and old can go see them. 2. A place fat guys shouldn't go because the animals might try to feed them.

Acknowledgments

Aber, James
Ajhar, Brian
Archinal, Jason
Biever, John
Berra, Yogi
Brett, George
Brinkley, David
Clay, Andrew Dice
Connors, Billy
Costner, Kevin
Cozzens, Steve
Crasnick, Jerry
Cullen, Les
Cutter, Brian
Dean, Dizzy
Dick, Dana
Doughty, Larry
Drago, Dick
Fingers, Rollie
Garagiola, Joe
Gower, Scott

Gustafson, Mike
Kennedy, Terry
Kornheiser, Tony
Jenkins, Bruce
Jones, Bill
KTXT – 88.1 FM
Lasorda, Tommy
Letterman, David
Luciano, Ron
Luksa, Frank
Major League Baseball
Mantle, Mickey
Mauch, Gene
Merrill, Stump
Miller, John
Nelson, Kevin
Otis, Amos
Peterson, Gary
Richards, Paul
Robinson, Bill
Robinson, Kelly

Rose, Pete
Sax, Steve
SHAPES Academy
Shearing, George
Sribhen, Arni
Smith, Bonnie
Snead, Bob
Sports Illustrated
Stengel, Casey
Stuart, Dick
Sullivan, Tim
Texas A&M Raggies
Texas Tech University
Thomas, Gorman
Tri-Star Pictures
Weaver, Earl
Williams, Ted
Winterrowd, Kirk
Paramount Pictures
Uptown Comedy Club
Zimmer, Don

Nelson, Kevin "Baseball's Even Greater Insults"
    Simon & Schuster, New York. © 1993
    223 pages. $9.00

Porcelay, James "Snaps: Playing the Dozens"
    Quill, William Morrow, New York. © 1993
    217 pages. $10.50

$\mathcal{A}$ppendix 1

The All-Brutal Team for 1995

Coaches–	Phil Claybaugh, Eastern New Mexico University
	Paul Kostacopolos, Providence College
	Todd Howey, West Texas A&M University
First Base	P. D. Neff, University of Nebraska, Kearney
Second Base	Captain Caveman, Grand Canyon University
Shortstop	Lane Supak, West Texas A&M University
Third Base	King Kong, Stanford University
Outfield	Tim Loefler, University of Texas
Outfield	Ben Bronson, Baylor University
Outfield	Ryan Bike, Providence College
Catcher	Matt Gancazs, Temple University
Designated Hitter	Duke Gonzales, Eastern New Mexico University
Pitcher	Todd Incanoloupo, Providence College
Pitcher	Brian Senterfit, University of Texas
Pitcher	Number 32, Baylor University
Pitcher	Ryan Kjos, Austin, University of Texas
Utility	Craig Farmer, Texas Christian University
Utility	Shea Morenz, University of Texas

Brutal Player of the Year
Lane Supak, West Texas A&M University

𝕬ppendix 2

The Brutality Conference

North Division
Providence
Temple
Mankato State
Nebraska-Kearney
Miami (Ohio)

South Division
Sul Ross State
Eastern New Mexico
College of the Southwest
Howard Payne
West Texas A&M University
Baylor University

Appendix 3

The Brutality Theorem

$$\frac{(-P)\ (-F)+(-H)}{(-C)}=Br^{2}$$

The Theorem states that a lack of pitching multiplied by a lack of fielding plus a lack of hitting divided by poor coaching is equal to Brutality Squared. Simply stated, teams of this quality are not very good and should be manhandled with relative ease. In some rare cases, referred to as the TEMPLE FACTOR, some teams continue to return to action as many as seven times in seven days to be beaten time and time again. It is apparent that this theorem is proven to be correct when the opponent displays a lack of pitching and/or offense. In any case, the end result is victory.

Appendix 4

Rules of Brutality

Temple Rule:
When two or more players touch the ball, the next one will drop it.

Miami (Ohio) Rule:
If any one player (other than the pitcher or catcher) touches the ball, they will drop it.

Providence Rule:
If in any game, the majority of errors originate in right field, then the Providence rule is in effect.

Stanford Rule:
If in any game a ball played by the Third Baseman is booted, the Stanford rule is in effect.